Our Civic Life
Rights and Responsibilities

by Lisa Moran

Table of Contents

Develop Language 2

CHAPTER 1 What Is a Citizen? 4
                Your Turn: Infer 9

CHAPTER 2 Our Rights 10
                Your Turn: Summarize 15

CHAPTER 3 Our Responsibilities 16
                Your Turn: Make Decisions 19

Career Explorations 20
Use Language to Restate 21
Social Studies Around You 22
Key Words 23
Index 24

DEVELOP LANGUAGE

People live in **communities**.
People can participate in a community in different ways.
They can share their ideas.
They can help others.

Talk about the photos with questions like these.

What are people doing?

The teacher is _____.

The _____ is _____.

The _____ are _____.

How are people helping others?

People are helping others by _____.

How do you participate in your community?

volunteers

2 Our Civic Life: Rights and Responsibilities

CHAPTER 1

What Is a Citizen?

The world has many **nations**, or countries.
Each nation has a **government**.
The leaders of the government make **laws**, or rules,
for people in that nation.

Each nation has **citizens**.
A citizen is a member of a nation.

Each nation has laws about becoming a citizen.
In the United States (U.S.), there are different ways to become a citizen.
You are a U.S. citizen if you were born in the United States.
You are a U.S. citizen if your parents are U.S. citizens.

▲ **A person born in the United States is a U.S. citizen.**

KEY IDEAS People are U.S. citizens if they are born in the United States. People are U.S. citizens if their parents are U.S. citizens.

Some people in the United States are not U.S. citizens.
They are citizens of other nations.
Many of them want to become U.S. citizens.
They can take a test.
They answer questions about our nation.
They promise to obey the laws of the United States.

▲ **New citizens promise to follow the laws of the United States.**

KEY IDEA People can take a test to become U.S. citizens.

U.S. citizens have special roles, or jobs.
One role is to participate in the government.
The United States government is a **democracy**.
In a democracy, the citizens choose their leaders.
The leaders make the laws.

▼ Some citizens want to be leaders. They ask other people to vote for them.

Explore Language
GREEK WORD ROOTS
democracy
demo (people) + *cracy* (rule) = rule of the people

KEY IDEAS In a democracy, the citizens choose their leaders. The leaders make the laws.

Chapter 1: What Is a Citizen? 7

The U.S. government has roles, too.
One important role is to protect the people.

How Does the U.S. Government Protect Us?

The Supreme Court protects our laws.

Firefighters protect our safety.

Soldiers protect us in time of war.

KEY IDEA An important role of the government is to protect the people.

YOUR TURN

INFER

In a democracy, citizens choose their leaders. Why is it important to choose good leaders?

It is important to choose good leaders because _____.

MAKE CONNECTIONS

Reread page 8. Think about your community. Who protects you in your community? Make a list of the people who protect you. Tell how they protect you.

USE THE LANGUAGE OF SOCIAL STUDIES

Who chooses the leaders in a democracy?

The citizens choose the leaders.

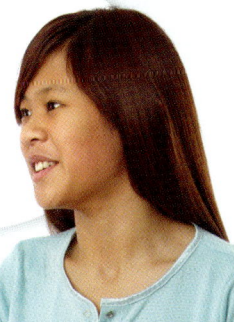

Chapter 1: What Is a Citizen?

CHAPTER 2

Our Rights

We have many freedoms in the United States.
We can live the way we choose.
We are free to choose our friends.
We are free to choose where we live.

These freedoms are our **rights**.
In the United States, everyone has rights.
The law protects our rights.
We can use our rights as long as we do not break any laws.

▲ In the United States, people are free to disagree with the government.

KEY IDEA A right is a freedom that the law protects.

Long ago, the leaders of the United States wrote the **Constitution**.
The Constitution tells how our government works.
Those leaders added the **Bill of Rights** to the Constitution.
The Bill of Rights protects our freedoms.

Bill of Rights

The original U.S. Constitution and Bill of Rights are kept in the National Archives in Washington, D.C.

The Bill of Rights protects our freedom to say what we think.
It protects our freedom to choose a religion.
It protects our freedom of assembly, or to meet with others.
It protects our freedom to publish the news.

	The Bill of Rights protects...	
✓	freedom of speech	
✓	freedom of religion	
✓	freedom of assembly	
✓	freedom of the press	

Sometimes a person breaks a law.
In other words, the person does not obey all the laws.
A trial is a way to decide if someone has broken a law.
The Bill of Rights protects our right to a fair trial.
The Bill of Rights protects other freedoms, too.

▼ **The Bill of Rights says that everyone has the right to a fair trial.**

KEY IDEA The Bill of Rights protects our freedoms.

14 *Our Civic Life: Rights and Responsibilities*

YOUR TURN

SUMMARIZE

Summarize what you learned in this chapter.

A right is _____.

Our rights include _____.

The Bill of Rights _____.

MAKE CONNECTIONS

Freedom of speech means that people can disagree with the government. People can talk about problems and ask for changes. How do people use their freedom of speech in your community? Give examples.

 STRATEGY FOCUS

Synthesize

Look again at the chart on page 13. Think about what you know about your rights. Explain why the Bill of Rights is an important document.

CHAPTER 3

We have a responsibility to obey traffic laws.

Our Responsibilities

All people in the United States have **responsibilities**.
Responsibilities are things that we must do, or should do.
For example, everyone must obey the laws.
Everyone must pay taxes.
Taxes are money that you pay to the government.

U.S. citizens have additional responsibilities.
Citizens should vote for their leaders.
Citizens should serve on juries.
A jury is a group of people in a trial.

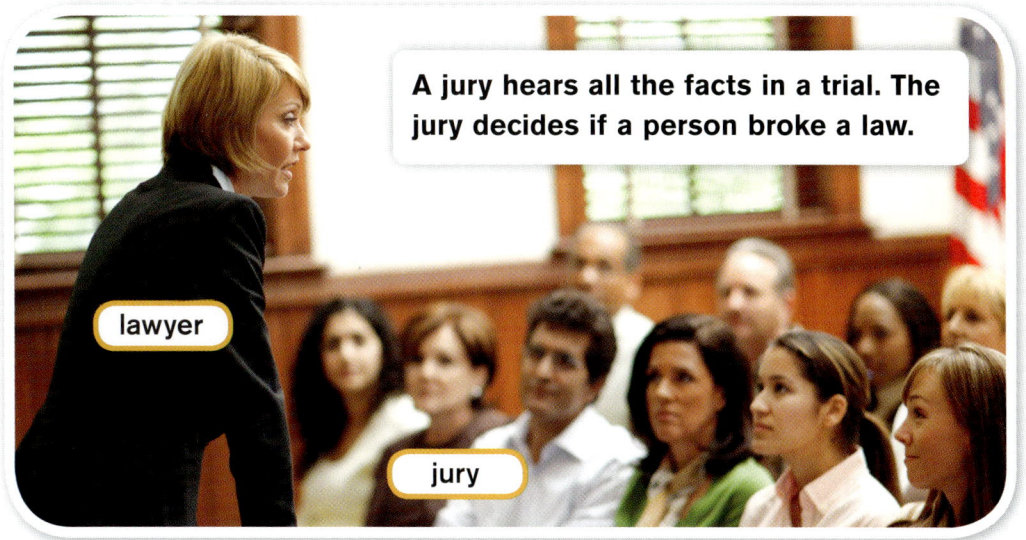

A jury hears all the facts in a trial. The jury decides if a person broke a law.

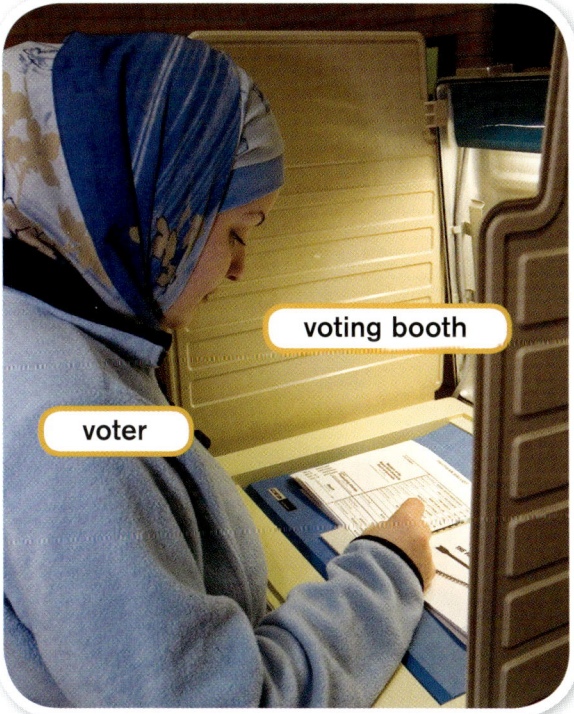

◀ Citizens vote to choose their leaders. Sometimes citizens vote on new laws.

KEY IDEAS

Everyone in the United States has responsibilities. U.S. citizens have additional responsibilities.

Chapter 3: Our Responsibilities

The U.S. government has responsibilities, too.
The government must obey the laws.
The government should use our tax money wisely.

How Does the Government Use Our Taxes?

to build roads and bridges

to protect us

to support education

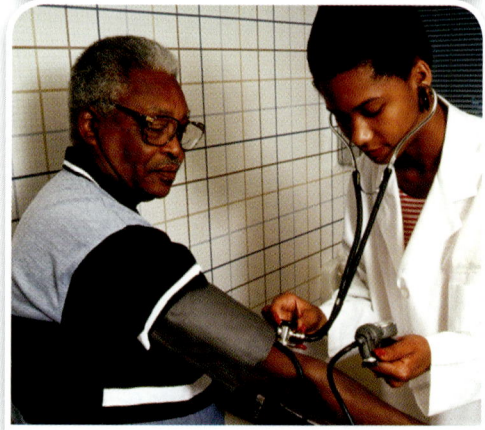

to support healthcare

KEY IDEA The U.S. government has responsibilities, too.

YOUR TURN

MAKE DECISIONS

Make a chart like this one. First, list at least five responsibilities of the U.S. government. Then decide which three responsibilities are the most important. Write them in the second column. Discuss how you made your decisions with a partner.

Responsibilities of the U.S. Government	My Top Three
• fix roads and bridges • support education	1. _____ 2. _____ 3. _____

MAKE CONNECTIONS

Everyone has responsibilities. What responsibilities do you have as a student? Make a list. Then make a list of your responsibilities as a family member.

EXPAND VOCABULARY

The word **right** has many meanings. Reread page 14. It tells about the Bill of Rights. Here are some other expressions that use the word **right**:

- **right** now
- all **right**
- the **right** answer

Tell the meaning of these expressions.
Then write your own sentence for each expression.

Chapter 3: Our Responsibilities

CAREER EXPLORATIONS

Police Officers: What Do They Do?

Police officers protect us by making sure that people obey our laws. Would you like to be a police officer? Find out more about this career.

▶ Police officers help in emergencies.

▲ Police officers find and arrest people who break the laws.

Our Civic Life: Rights and Responsibilities

USE LANGUAGE TO RESTATE

Words that Restate

When you restate something, you say the same thing with different words. You can use the phrase **this means that** to restate something. You can also use **in other words**.

EXAMPLE

The Bill of Rights gives us the freedom to assemble.

This means that the Bill of Rights gives us the freedom to meet with others.

Talk About It

With a partner, look at the photos in this book. Describe a photo that shows a freedom that we have. Then restate each other's ideas in your own words.

Write a Restatement

Choose a Key Idea in this book. Restate the Key Idea in your own words.

- First, state the Key Idea.
- Then restate the Key Idea in your own words.
- Give examples to show what you mean.

Words You Can Use
This means that...
In other words...
or

SOCIAL STUDIES AROUND YOU

Freedom of the Press

In the United States, newspapers can write what they want as long as they do not break the law.
This is freedom of the press.

Look at the newspapers above.
Answer the questions.

What are the stories about?

Why is it important that people can write what they want?

Key Words

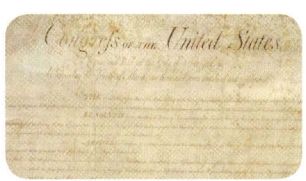

Bill of Rights the part of the Constitution that lists our rights
The **Bill of Rights** protects our right to a fair trial.

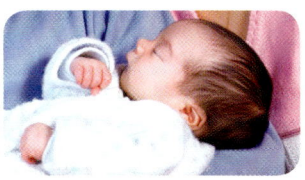

citizen (citizens) a member of a nation
A person born in the United States is a U.S. **citizen**.

Constitution the document that tells how the U.S. government works
Leaders wrote the U.S. **Constitution** many years ago.

democracy (democracies) a government in which citizens vote for their leaders
The United States is a **democracy**.

government (governments) a system through which some people rule others
The **government** makes laws for people and protects people's rights.

right (rights) something we are free to do
We have a **right** to choose where we live.

responsibility (responsibilities) something a person must do, or should do
We have a **responsibility** to pay taxes.

Index

Bill of Rights 12–14, 15
citizen 4–7, 9, 11, 18, 19
community 4–5, 19
Constitution 12, 15
democracy 7, 9
freedom 13–14, 15
government 4–8, 9, 11, 16, 18, 19
jury 18, 19
responsibility 16–18, 19
right 10–14, 15, 16, 19
role 7–8
services 8, 9, 17
tax 17, 19
trial 14, 18, 19, 20
vote 18, 19

MILLMARK EDUCATION CORPORATION
Ericka Markman, President and CEO; Karen Peratt, VP, Editorial Director; Lisa Bingen, VP, Marketing; Dave Willette, VP, Sales; Rachel L. Moir, VP, Operations and Production; Shelby Alinsky, Associate Editor; Ana Nuncio, Language Editor; Hanneman Productions, Photo Research; Arleen Nakama, Technology Projects

PROGRAM AUTHORS
Mary Hawley, Program Author, Instructional Design
Peggy Altoff, Program Author, Social Studies

STUDENT BOOK DEVELOPMENT Gare Thompson Associates, Inc.

BOOK DESIGN Steve Curtis Design

TECHNOLOGY Six Red Marbles

CONTENT REVIEWER
Margit McGuire, PhD, Program Director and Professor of Teacher Education, Seattle University, Seattle, WA

PROGRAM ADVISORS
Scott K. Baker, PhD, Pacific Institutes for Research, Eugene, OR
Carla C. Johnson, EdD, University of Toledo, Toledo, OH
Margit McGuire, PhD, Seattle University, Seattle, WA
Donna Ogle, EdD, National-Louis University, Chicago, IL
Betty Ansin Smallwood, PhD, Center for Applied Linguistics, Washington, DC
Gail Thompson, PhD, Claremont Graduate University, Claremont, CA
Emma Violand-Sánchez, EdD, Arlington Public Schools, Arlington, VA (retired)

PHOTO CREDITS Cover ©James Steidl/Shutterstock; IFC and 15b ©David Safanda/iStockphoto.com; 1a ©JustASC/Shutterstock; 2a ©Jonathan Nourok/PhotoEdit; 2-3a and 8c ©Mark Richards/Photo Edit; 3a, 4a, 18c ©Michael Newman/Photo Edit; 3b ©Tom McCarthy/Photo Edit; 5a ©GoGo Images/Photolibrary; 6a ©AP Photo/Chitose Suzuki; 7a ©Bob Daemmrich/Photo Edit; 8a ©Rudy Sulgan/age fotostock; 8b ©Shari L. Morris/age fotostock; 9a ©AP Photo; 9b and 9c ©Photos by Ken Karp; 10a ©Myrleen Ferguson Cate/Photo Edit; 11a ©Catherine Jones/Shutterstock; 12a and 23a ©National Archives I Reference Section, Textual Archives Services Division, Washington, DC; 12b ©Michael Ventura/Alamy; 13a ©AP Photo/Dale Sparks; 13b ©Visions of America, LLC/Alamy; 13c ©AP Photo/Sue Ogrocki; 13d ©Jeff Greenberg/Photo Edit; 14a ©Billy E. Barnes/Photo Edit; 15a ©AP Photo/Dave Weaver; 16a ©Richard Levine/Alamy; 17a ©Corbis/Photolibrary; 17b ©Jim West/PhotoEdit; 18a ©Imagestate/agefotostock; 18b ©Dennis MacDonald/age fotostock; 18d Merritt Vincent/Photo Edit; 20a ©AP Photo/Buffalo News, Michael Groll; 20b ©AP Photo/The Citizens' Voice, Mark Moran; 22a ©David Young-Wolff/Photo Edit; 23b ©Bubbles Photolibrary/Alamy; 23c ©Mark R/Shutterstock; 23d ©Jim West/Alamy; 23e ©Gary Blakeley/Shutterstock; 23f ©Feverpitch/Shutterstock; 23g ©Mr. B Hughes/Shutterstock; 24a ©Monkey Business Images/Shutterstock

Copyright ©2009 Millmark Education Corporation

All rights reserved. Reproduction of the whole or any part of the contents without written permission from the publisher is prohibited. Millmark Education and ConceptLinks are registered trademarks of Millmark Education Corporation.

Published by Millmark Education Corporation
PO Box 30829
Bethesda, MD 20824

ISBN-13: 978-1-4334-0690-4

Printed in the USA

10 9 8 7 6 5 4 3 2 1

Our Civic Life: Rights and Responsibilities